Thomas Bailey Aldrich

Later lyrics selected from Mercedes, The sisters' tragedy,

Wyndham towers and Unguarded gates

Thomas Bailey Aldrich

Later lyrics selected from Mercedes, The sisters' tragedy, Wyndham towers and Unguarded gates

ISBN/EAN: 9783743328242

Manufactured in Europe, USA, Canada, Australia, Japa

Cover: Foto ©ninafisch / pixelio.de

Manufactured and distributed by brebook publishing software (www.brebook.com)

Thomas Bailey Aldrich

Later lyrics selected from Mercedes, The sisters' tragedy,

Wyndham towers and Unguarded gates

T. B. ALDRICH

Later Lyrics

SELECTED FROM

MERCEDES
THE SISTERS' TRAGEDY
WYNDHAM TOWERS

AND

UNGUARDED GATES

BOSTON AND NEW YORK
HOUGHTON, MIFFLIN AND COMPANY
The Riverside Press, Cambridge
1896

IN MEMORIAM

The Riverside Press, Cambridge:
Electrotyped and Printed by H. O. Houghton & Co.

I would be the Lyric
   Ever on the lip,
Rather than the Epic
   Memory lets slip.
I would be the diamond
   At my lady's ear,
Rather than the June-rose
   Worn but once a year.

CONTENTS

		PAGE
Sweetheart, sigh no more		11
Memory		13
A Touch of Nature		14
Alec Yeaton's Son		16
Invita Minerva		19
Insomnia		20
Threnody		22
"Pillared Arch and Sculptured Tower"		24
At Nijnii-Novgorod		25
The Winter Robin		27
Echo-Song		28
A Mood		30
Sargent's Portrait of Edwin Booth at "The Players"		31
Thorwaldsen		33
Guilielmus Rex		34
A Bridal Measure		35
Imogen		37

"Like Crusoe, walking by the lonely strand" 38

Batuschka 39

A Dedication 41

Soldiers' Song 42

Apparitions 44

Prescience 45

Tennyson 47

"When from the tense chords of that mighty lyre" 49

Outward Bound 51

Heredity 53

The Sailing of the Autocrat 54

Pepita 56

Books and Seasons 60

Discipline 62

The Letter 63

On Lynn Terrace 64

Andromeda 68

"I'll not confer with Sorrow" 70

No Songs in Winter 71

Two Moods 72

Andalusian Cradle-Song 74

The Voice of the Sea 76

"I vex me not with brooding on the years" 77

CONTENTS 9

A Serenade 79
A Refrain 81
"Great Captain, glorious in our wars " . 82
Reminiscence 84
Broken Music 85
Comedy 88
Seeming Defeat 89
A Petition 91
Quits 92

LATER LYRICS

I

SWEETHEART, SIGH NO MORE

IT was with doubt and trembling
I whispered in her ear.
Go, take her answer, bird-on-bough,
That all the world may hear —
  Sweetheart, sigh no more!

Sing it, sing it, tawny throat,
Upon the wayside tree,
How fair she is, how true she is,
How dear she is to me —
  Sweetheart, sigh no more!

Sing it, sing it, tawny throat,
And through the summer long

The winds among the clover-tops,
And brooks, for all their silvery stops,
Shall envy you the song —
Sweetheart, sigh no more!

II

MEMORY

My mind lets go a thousand things,
Like dates of wars and deaths of kings,
And yet recalls the very hour —
'T was noon by yonder village tower,
And on the last blue noon in May —
The wind came briskly up this way,
Crisping the brook beside the road;
Then, pausing here, set down its load
Of pine-scents, and shook listlessly
Two petals from that wild-rose tree.

13

A TOUCH OF NATURE

WHEN first the crocus thrusts its point
    of gold
Up through the still snow-drifted garden-
    mould,
And folded green things in dim woods
    unclose
Their crinkled spears, a sudden tremor
    goes
Into my veins and makes me kith and
    kin
To every wild-born thing that thrills and
    blows.
Sitting beside this crumbling sea-coal
    fire,
Here in the city's ceaseless roar and din,
Far from the brambly paths I used to
    know,
Far from the rustling brooks that slip
    and shine

Where the Neponset alders take their
    glow,
I share the tremulous sense of bud and
    briar
And inarticulate ardors of the vine.

ALEC YEATON'S SON

GLOUCESTER, AUGUST, 1720

THE wind it wailed, the wind it moaned,
  And the white caps flecked the sea ;
"An' I would to God," the skipper
    groaned,
  " I had not my boy with me ! "

Snug in the stern-sheets, little John
  Laughed as the scud swept by ;
But the skipper's sunburnt cheek grew
    wan
  As he watched the wicked sky.

"Would he were at his mother's side ! "
  And the skipper's eyes were dim.
" Good Lord in heaven, if ill betide,
  What would become of him !

" For me — my muscles are as steel,
  For me let hap what may ;

I might make shift upon the keel
　　Until the break o' day.

"But he, he is so weak and small,
　　So young, scarce learned to stand —
O pitying Father of us all,
　　I trust him in Thy hand!

"For Thou who markest from on high
　　A sparrow's fall — each one! —
Surely, O Lord, thou 'lt have an eye
　　On Alec Yeaton's son!"

Then, helm hard-port; right straight he
　　　　sailed
　　Towards the headland light:
The wind it moaned, the wind it wailed,
　　And black, black fell the night.

Then burst a storm to make one quail,
　　Though　housed　from　winds　and
　　　　waves —
They who could tell about that gale
　　Must rise from watery graves!

Sudden it came, as sudden went;
　　Ere half the night was sped,

The winds were hushed, the waves
    were spent,
  And the stars shone overhead.

Now, as the morning mist grew thin,
  The folk on Gloucester shore
Saw a little figure floating in
  Secure, on a broken oar!

Up rose the cry, " A wreck! a wreck!
  Pull, mates, and waste no breath!" —
They knew it, though 't was but a speck
  Upon the edge of death!

Long did they marvel in the town
  At God his strange decree,
That let the stalwart skipper drown
  And the little child go free!

V

INVITA MINERVA

NOT of Desire alone is music born,
Not till the Muse wills is our passion
    crowned;
Unsought she comes; if sought but sel-
    dom found,
Repaying thus our longing with her
    scorn.
Hence is it poets often are forlorn,
In super-subtle chains of silence bound,
And mid the crowds that compass them
    around
Still dwell in isolation night and morn,
With knitted brow and cheek all pas-
    sion-pale
Showing the baffled purpose of the mind.
Hence is it I, that find no prayers avail
To move my Lyric Mistress to be kind,
Have stolen away into this leafy dale,
Drawn by the flutings of the silvery
    wind.

VI

INSOMNIA

SLUMBER, hasten down this way,
    And, ere midnight dies,
Silence lay upon my lips,
    Darkness on my eyes.

Send me a fantastic dream;
    Fashion me afresh;
Into some celestial thing
    Change this mortal flesh.

Well I know one may not choose;
    One is helpless still
In the purple realm of Sleep:
    Use me as you will.

Let me be a frozen pine
    In dead glacier lands;
Let me pant, a leopard stretched
    On the Libyan sands.

20

Silver fin or scarlet wing
    Grant me, either one;
Sink me deep in emerald glooms,
    Lift me to the sun.

Or of me a gargoyle make,
    Face of ape or gnome,
Such as frights the tavern-boor
    Reeling drunken home.

Work on me your own caprice,
    Give me any shape;
Only, Slumber, from myself
    Let myself escape!

VII

THRENODY

I

UPON your hearse this flower I lay.
Brief be your sleep! You shall be
known
When lesser men have had their day:
Fame blossoms where true seed is sown,
Or soon or late, let Time wrong what it
may.

II

Unvext by any dream of fame,
You smiled, and bade the world pass
by :
But I — I turned, and saw a name
Shaping itself against the sky —
White star that rose amid the battle's
flame!

III

Brief be your sleep, for I would see
Your laurels — ah, how trivial now
To him must earthly laurel be
Who wears the amaranth on his brow !
How vain the voices of mortality !

"PILLARED ARCH AND SCULP-
TURED TOWER"

PILLARED arch and sculptured tower
Of Ilium have had their hour;
The dust of many a king is blown
On the winds from zone to zone;
Many a warrior sleeps unknown.
Time and Death hold each in thrall,
Yet is Love the lord of all;
Still does Helen's beauty stir
Because a poet sang of her!

24

AT NIJNII–NOVGOROD

" A CRAFTY Persian set this stone ;
   A dusk Sultana wore it ;
And from her slender finger, sir,
   A ruthless Arab tore it.

" A ruby, like a drop of blood —
   That deep-in tint that lingers
And seems to melt, perchance was
      caught
   From those poor mangled fingers !

" A spendthrift got it from the knave,
   And tost it, like a blossom,
That night into a dancing-girl's
   Accurst and balmy bosom.

" And so it went.   One day a Jew
   At Cairo chanced to spy it

Amid a one-eyed peddler's pack,
 And did not care to buy it —

"Yet bought it all the same.   You see,
 The Jew he knew a jewel.
He bought it cheap to sell it dear :
 The ways of trade are cruel.

"But I — be Allah's all the praise ! —
 Such avarice, I scoff it!
If I buy cheap, why, I sell cheap,
 Content with modest profit.

"This ring — such chasing ! look, milord,
 What workmanship !   By Heaven,
The price I name you makes the thing
 As if the thing were given !

"A stone without a flaw !   A queen
 Might not disdain to wear it.
Three hundred roubles buys the stone ;
 No kopeck less, I swear it ! "

Thus Hassan, holding up the ring
 To me, no eager buyer. —
A hundred roubles was not much
 To pay so sweet a liar !

THE WINTER ROBIN

Sursum corda

Now is that sad time of year
When no flower or leaf is here;
When in misty Southern ways
Oriole and jay have flown,
And of all sweet birds, alone
The robin stays.

So give thanks at Christmas-tide:
Hopes of spring-time yet abide!
See, in spite of darksome days,
Wind and rain and bitter chill,
Snow and sleet-hung branches, still
The robin stays!

27

ECHO-SONG

I

WHO can say where Echo dwells?
In some mountain-cave, methinks,
Where the white owl sits and blinks;
Or in deep sequestered dells,
Where the foxglove hangs its bells,
Echo dwells.
Echo!
Echo!

II

Phantom of the crystal air,
Daughter of sweet Mystery!
Here is one has need of thee;
Lead him to thy secret lair,
Myrtle brings he for thy hair —
Hear his prayer,
Echo!
Echo!

III

Echo, lift thy drowsy head,
  And repeat each charmèd word
  Thou must needs have overheard
Yestere'en ere, rosy-red,
Daphne down the valley fled —
            Words unsaid,
              Echo!
                Echo!

IV

Breathe the vows she since denies!
  She hath broken every vow;
  What she would she would not now —
Thou didst hear her perjuries.
Whisper, whilst I shut my eyes,
            Those sweet lies,
              Echo!
                Echo!

A MOOD

A BLIGHT, a gloom, I know not what,
    has crept upon my gladness —
Some vague, remote ancestral touch of
    sorrow, or of madness;
A fear that is not fear, a pain that has
    not pain's insistence;
A sense of longing, or of loss, in some
    foregone existence;
A subtle hurt that never pen has writ
    nor tongue has spoken —
Such hurt perchance as Nature feels
    when a blossomed bough is broken.

30

SARGENT'S PORTRAIT OF ED-WIN BOOTH AT "THE PLAY-ERS"

THAT face which no man ever saw
And from his memory banished quite,
With eyes in which are Hamlet's awe
And Cardinal Richelieu's subtle light,
Looks from this frame. A master's hand
Has set the master-player here,
In the fair temple that he planned
Not for himself. To us most dear
This image of him! " It was thus
He looked; such pallor touched his
    cheek;
With that same grace he greeted us —
Nay, 't is the man, could it but speak! "
Sad words that shall be said some day —
Far fall the day! O cruel Time,
Whose breath sweeps mortal things
    away,

Spare long this image of his prime,
That others standing in the place
Where, save as ghosts, we come no more,
May know what sweet majestic face
The gentle Prince of Players wore!

THORWALDSEN

NOT in the fabled influence of some
    star,
Benign or evil, do our fortunes lie:
We are the arbiters of destiny,
Lords of the life we either make or mar.
We are our own impediment and bar
To noble issues. With averted eye
We let the golden moment pass us by,
Time's foolish spendthrifts, searching
    wide and far
For what lies close at hand. To serve
    our turn
We ask fair wind and favorable tide.
From the dead Danish sculptor let us
    learn
To make Occasion, not to be denied:
Against the sheer precipitous mountain-
    side
Thorwaldsen carved his Lion at Lucerne.

GUILIELMUS REX

THE folk who lived in Shakespeare's day
And saw that gentle figure pass
By London Bridge, his frequent way —
They little knew what man he was.

The pointed beard, the courteous mien,
The equal port to high and low,
All this they saw or might have seen —
But not the light behind the brow !

The doublet's modest gray or brown,
The slender sword-hilt's plain device,
What sign had these for prince or clown ?
Few turned, or none, to scan him twice.

Yet 't was the king of England's kings !
The rest with all their pomps and trains
Are mouldered, half-remembered things—
'T is he alone that lives and reigns !

A BRIDAL MEASURE

FOR S. F.

Gifts they sent her manifold,
Diamonds and pearls and gold.
One there was among the throng
Had not Midas' touch at need:
He against a sylvan reed
Set his lips and breathed a song.

Bid bright Flora, as she comes,
Snatch a spray of orange blooms
    For a maiden's hair.
Let the Hours their aprons fill
With mignonette and daffodil,
    And all that's fair.

For her bosom fetch the rose
    That is rarest —
Not that either these or those

Could by any happening be
Ornaments to such as she;
They 'll but show, when she is dressed,
She is fairer than the fairest
And out-betters what is best!

IMOGEN

LEONATUS POSTHUMUS *speaks:*

SORROW, make a verse for me
  That shall breathe all human grieving;
Let it be love's exequy,
  And the knell of all believing!
Let it such sweet pathos have
As a violet on a grave,
  Or a dove's moan when his mate
  Leaves the new nest desolate.
Sorrow, Sorrow, by this token,
Braid a wreath for Beauty's head. . . .
  Valley-lilies, one or two,
  Should be woven with the rue.
Sorrow, Sorrow, all is spoken —
  She is dead!

"LIKE CRUSOE, WALKING BY THE LONELY STRAND"

LIKE Crusoe, walking by the lonely
    strand
And seeing a human footprint on the
    sand,
Have I this day been startled, finding
    here,
Set in brown mould and delicately clear,
Spring's footprint — the first crocus of
    the year !
O sweet invasion ! Farewell solitude !
Soon shall wild creatures of the field and
    wood
Flock from all sides with much ado and
    stir,
And make of me most willing prisoner !

XIX

BATUSCHKA[1]

FROM yonder gilded minaret
Beside the steel-blue Neva set,
I faintly catch, from time to time,
The sweet, aerial midnight chime —
    "God save the Tsar!"

Above the ravelins and the moats
Of the white citadel it floats;
And men in dungeons far beneath
Listen, and pray, and gnash their teeth —
    "God save the Tsar!"

The soft reiterations sweep
Across the horror of their sleep,
As if some dæmon in his glee

---

[1] "Little Father," or "Dear Little Father," a
term of endearment applied to the Tsar in Russian folk-song.

Were mocking at their misery —
   "God save the Tsar!"

In his Red Palace over there,
Wakeful, he needs must hear the prayer.
How can it drown the broken cries
Wrung from his children's agonies? —
   "God save the Tsar!"

Father they called him from of old —
Batuschka! . . . How his heart is cold!
Wait till a million scourgèd men
Rise in their awful might, and then —
   God save the Tsar!

A DEDICATION

TAKE these rhymes into thy grace,
    Since they are of thy begetting,
Lady, that dost make each place
    Where thou art a jewel's setting.

Some such glamour lend this Book:
    Let it be thy poet's wages
That henceforth thy gracious look
    Lies reflected on its pages.

XXI

SOLDIERS' SONG

(FROM "MERCEDES")

THE camp is hushed; the fires burn low;
Like ghosts the sentries come and go:
Now seen, now lost, upon the height
A keen drawn sabre glimmers white.
Swiftly the midnight steals away —
 Reposez-vous, bons chevaliers!

Perchance into your dream shall come
Visions of love or thoughts of home;
The furtive night wind, hurrying by,
Shall kiss away the half-breathed sigh,
And softly whispering, seem to say,
 Reposez-vous, bons chevaliers!

Through star-lit dusk and shimmering
  dew
It is your lady comes to you!

Delphine, Lisette, Annette — who knows
By what sweet wayward name she goes?
Wrapped in white arms till break of day,
Reposez-vous, bons chevaliers!

XXII

APPARITIONS

At noon of night, and at the night's pale
end,
Such things have chanced to me
As one, by day, would scarcely tell a
friend
For fear of mockery.

Shadows, you say, mirages of the brain!
I know not, faith, not I.
Is it more strange the dead should walk
again
Than that the quick should die?

44

XXIII

PRESCIENCE

THE new moon hung in the sky,
  The sun was low in the west,
And my betrothed and I
  In the churchyard paused to rest —
    Happy maiden and lover,
    Dreaming the old dream over:
The light winds wandered by,
  And robins chirped from the nest.

And lo! in the meadow-sweet
  Was the grave of a little child,
With a crumbling stone at the feet,
  And the ivy running wild —
    Tangled ivy and clover
    Folding it over and over:
Close to my sweetheart's feet
  Was the little mound up-piled.

45

Stricken with nameless fears,
   She shrank and clung to me,
And her eyes were filled with tears
   For a sorrow I did not see:
      Lightly the winds were blowing,
      Softly her tears were flowing —
Tears for the unknown years
   And a sorrow that was to be!

XXIV

TENNYSON

1890

I

SHAKESPEARE and Milton — what third
blazoned name
Shall lips of after ages link to these?
His who, beside the wild encircling
seas,
Was England's voice, her voice with one
acclaim,
For threescore years; whose word of
praise was fame,
Whose scorn gave pause to man's
iniquities.

II

What strain was his in that Crimean
war?
A bugle-call in battle; a low breath,
Plaintive and sweet, above the fields of
death!

So year by year the music rolled afar,
From Euxine wastes to flowery Kanda-
        har,
    Bearing the laurel or the cypress
        wreath.

III

Others shall have their little space of
        time,
    Their proper niche and bust, then fade
        away
    Into the darkness, poets of a day;
But thou, O builder of enduring rhyme,
Thou shalt not pass!   Thy fame in
        every clime
    On earth shall live where Saxon speech
        has sway.

IV

Waft me this verse across the winter sea,
    Through light and dark, through mist
        and blinding sleet,
    O winter winds, and lay it at his feet;
Though the poor gift betray my poverty,
At his feet lay it: it may chance that he
    Will find no gift, where reverence is,
        unmeet.

"WHEN FROM THE TENSE CHORDS OF THAT MIGHTY LYRE"

January, 1892

I

WHEN from the tense chords of that
    mighty lyre
  The Master's hand, relaxing, falls
    away,
    And those rich strings are silent for
    all time,
Then shall Love pine, and Passion lack
    her fire,
And Faith seem voiceless. Man to
    man shall say,
    " Dead is the last of England's lords
    of rhyme."

II

Yet — stay! there 's one, a later laureled
    brow,
  With purple blood of poets in his veins;
    Him has the Muse claimed; him
    might Marlowe own;
Greek Sappho's son! — men's praises
    seek him now.
  Happy the realm where one such voice
    remains!
    His the dropt wreath and the unen-
    vied throne.

III

The wreath the world gives, not the
    mimic wreath
  That chance might make the gift of
    king or queen.
    O finder of undreamed-of harmonies!
Since Shelley's lips were hushed by cruel
    death,
  What lyric voice so sweet as this has
    been
    Borne to us on the winds from over
    seas?

XXVI

OUTWARD BOUND

I LEAVE behind me the elm-shadowed
    square
And carven portals of the silent street,
And wander on with listless, vagrant
    feet
Through seaward-leading alleys, till the
    air
Smells of the sea, and straightway then
    the care
Slips from my heart, and life once more
    is sweet.
At the lane's ending lie the white-winged
    fleet.
O restless Fancy, whither wouldst thou
    fare?
Here are brave pinions that shall take
    thee far —
Gaunt hulks of Norway; ships of red
    Ceylon;

Slim-masted lovers of the blue Azores!
'T is but an instant hence to Zanzibar,
Or to the regions of the Midnight Sun:
Ionian isles are thine, and all the fairy
      shores!

XXVII

HEREDITY

A soldier of the Cromwell stamp,
With sword and psalm-book by his side
At home alike in church and camp:
Austere he lived, and smileless died.

But she, a creature soft and fine —
From Spain, some say, some say from
        France:
Within her veins leapt blood like wine —
She led her Roundhead lord a dance!

In Grantham church they lie asleep;
Just where, the verger may not know.
Strange that two hundred years should
        keep
The old ancestral fires aglow!

In me these two have met again;
To each my nature owes a part:
To one, the cool and reasoning brain;
To one, the quick, unreasoning heart.

53

XXVIII

THE SAILING OF THE AUTO-CRAT

ON BOARD THE S. S. CEPHALONIA, APRIL
26, 1886

I

O WIND and Wave, be kind to him!
So, Wave and Wind, we give thee
thanks!
O Fog, that from Newfoundland Banks
Makest the blue bright ocean dim,
Delay him not!   And ye who snare
The wayworn shipman with your song,
Go pipe your ditties otherwhere
While this brave vessel plows along!
If still to lure him be your thought,
O phantoms of the watery zone,
Be wary lest yourselves get caught
With music sweeter than your own!

54

II

Yet, soft sea spirits, be not mute ;
Murmur about the prow, and make
Melodious the west wind's lute.
For him may radiant mornings break
From out the bosom of the deep,
And golden noons above him bend,
And fortunate constellations keep
Bright vigils to his journey's end !

III

Take him, green Erin, to thy breast!
Keep him, gray London — for a while !
In him we send thee of our best,
Our wisest word, our blithest smile —
Our epigram, alert and pat,
That kills with joy the folly hit —
Our Yankee Tsar, our Autocrat
Of all the happy realms of wit !
Take him and keep him — but forbear
To keep him more than half a year. . . .
His presence will be sunshine there,
His absence will be shadow here !

PEPITA

SCARCELY sixteen years old
  Is Pepita.   (You understand,
  A breath of this sunny land
Turns green fruit into gold :

A maiden's conscious blood
  In the cheek of girlhood glows ;
  A bud slips into a rose
Before it is quite a bud.)

And I in Seville — sedate,
  An American, with an eye
  For that strip of indigo sky
Half-glimpsed through a Moorish gate —

I see her, sitting up there,
  With tortoise-shell comb and fan ;
  Red-lipped, but a trifle wan,
Because of her coal-black hair ;

And the hair a trifle dull,
  Because of the eyes beneath,
  And the radiance of her teeth
When her smile is at its full.

Against the balcony rail
  She leans, and looks on the street;
  Her lashes, long and discreet,
Shading her eyes like a veil.

Held by a silver dart,
  The mantilla's delicate lace
  Falls each side of her face
And crosswise over her heart.

This is Pepita — this
  Her hour for taking her ease:
  A lover under the trees
In the *calle* were not amiss!

Well, I must needs pass by,
  With a furtive glance, be it said,
  At the dusk Murillo head
And the Andalusian eye.

In the Plaza I hear the sounds
  Of guitar and castanet;

Although it is early yet,
The dancers are on their rounds.

Softly the sunlight falls
  On the slim Giralda tower,
  That now peals forth the hour
O'er broken ramparts and walls.

Ah, what glory and gloom
  In this Arab-Spanish town!
  What masonry, golden-brown,
And hung with tendril and bloom!

Place of forgotten kings! —
  With fountains that never play,
  And gardens where day by day
The lonely cicada sings.

Traces are everywhere
  Of the dusky race that came,
  And passed, like a sudden flame,
Leaving their sighs in the air!

Taken with things like these,
  Pepita fades out of my mind:
  Pleasure enough I find
In Moorish column and frieze.

And yet I have my fears,
  If this had been long ago,
  I might . . . well, I do not know . . .
She with her sixteen years !

XXX

BOOKS AND SEASONS

BECAUSE the sky is blue; because blithe
      May
Masks in the wren's note and the lilac's
      hue ;
Because — in fine, because the sky is blue
I will read none but piteous tales to-day.
Keep happy laughter till the skies be
      gray,
And the sad season cypress wears, and
      rue ;
Then, when the wind is moaning in the
      flue,
And ways are dark, bid Chaucer make us
      gay.
But now a little sadness !   All too sweet
This springtide riot, this most poignant
      air,

This sensuous sphere of color and per-
fume !
So listen, love, while I the woes repeat
Of Hamlet and Ophelia, and that pair
Whose bridal bed was builded in a tomb.

DISCIPLINE

In the crypt at the foot of the stairs
They lay there, a score of the Dead:
They could hear the priest at his prayers,
And the litany overhead.

They knew when the great crowd stirred
As the Host was lifted on high;
And they smiled in the dark when they
      heard
Some light-footed nun trip by.

Side by side on their shelves
For years and years they lay;
And those who misbehaved themselves
Had their coffin-plates taken away.

Thus is the legend told
In black-letter monkish rhyme,
Explaining those plaques of gold
That vanished from time to time!

THE LETTER

EDWARD ROWLAND SILL, DIED FEBRUARY 27,
1887

I HELD his letter in my hand,
  And even while I read
The lightning flashed across the land
  The word that he was dead.

How strange it seemed! His living voice
  Was speaking from the page
Those courteous phrases, tersely choice,
  Light-hearted, witty, sage.

I wondered what it was that died!
  The man himself was here,
His modesty, his scholar's pride,
  His soul serene and clear.

These neither death nor time shall dim,
  Still this sad thing must be —
Henceforth I may not speak to him,
  Though he can speak to me!

ON LYNN TERRACE

ALL day to watch the blue wave curl and
 break,
  All night to hear it plunging on the
   shore —
In this sea-dream such draughts of life I
 take,
    I cannot ask for more.

Behind me lie the idle life and vain,
  The task unfinished, and the weary
   hours;
That long wave softly bears me back to
 Spain
    And the Alhambra's towers.

Once more I halt in Andalusian pass,
  To list the mule-bells jingling on the
   height;
Below, against the dull esparto grass,
    The almonds glimmer white.

Huge gateways, wrinkled, with rich grays
  and browns,
  Invite my fancy, and I wander through
The gable-shadowed, zigzag streets of
  towns
    The world's first sailors knew.

Or, if I will, from out this thin sea-
  haze
  Low-lying cliffs of lovely Calais rise ;
Or yonder, with the pomp of olden days,
    Venice salutes my eyes.

Or some gaunt castle lures me up its
  stair ;
  I see, far off, the red-tiled hamlets
  shine,
And catch, through slits of windows here
  and there,
    Blue glimpses of the Rhine.

Again I pass Norwegian fjord and fell,
  And through bleak wastes to where
  the sunset's fires
Light up the white-walled Russian cita-
.   del,
    The Kremlin's domes and spires.

And now I linger in green English lanes,
  By garden - plots of rose and helio-
    trope;
And now I face the sudden pelting rains
  On some lone Alpine slope.

Now at Tangier, among the packed ba-
    zaars,
  I saunter, and the merchants at the
    doors
Smile, and entice me: here are jewels
    like stars,
      And curved knives of the Moors;

Cloths of Damascus, strings of amber
    dates;
  What would Howadji . . . silver, gold,
    or stone?
Prone on the sun-scorched plain outside
    the gates
      The camels make their moan.

All this is mine, as I lie dreaming here,
  High on the windy terrace, day by
    day;
And mine the children's laughter, sweet
    and clear,
      Ringing across the bay.

For me the clouds; the ships sail by for
    me;
For me the petulant sea-gull takes its
    flight;
And mine the tender moonrise on the sea,
    And hollow caves of night.

XXXIV

ANDROMEDA

THE smooth-worn coin and threadbare
    classic phrase
Of Grecian myths that did beguile my
    youth,
Beguile me not as in the olden days:
I think more grief and beauty dwell with
    truth.
Andromeda, in fetters by the sea,
Star-pale with anguish till young Perseus
    came,
Less moves me with her suffering than
    she,
The slim girl figure fettered to dark
    shame,
That nightly haunts the park, there, like
    a shade,
Trailing her wretchedness from street to
    street.

68

See where she passes — neither wife nor
    maid.
How all mere fiction crumbles at her feet !
Here is woe's self, and not the mask of
    woe :
A legend's shadow shall not move you so !

XXXV

"I 'LL NOT CONFER WITH SORROW"

I 'LL not confer with Sorrow
    Till to-morrow;
But Joy shall have her way
    This very day.

Ho, eglantine and cresses
    For her tresses! —
Let Care, the beggar, wait
    Outside the gate.

Tears if you will — but after
    Mirth and laughter;
Then, folded hands on breast
    And endless rest.

70

XXXVI

NO SONGS IN WINTER

THE sky is gray as gray may be,
There is no bird upon the bough,
There is no leaf on vine or tree.

In the Neponset marshes now
Willow-stems, rosy in the wind,
Shiver with hidden sense of snow.

So, too, 't is winter in my mind,
No light-winged fancy comes and stays:
A season churlish and unkind.

Slow creep the hours, slow creep the days,
The black ink crusts upon the pen —
Wait till the bluebirds, wrens, and jays,
And golden orioles come again!

71

XXXVII

TWO MOODS

I

BETWEEN the budding and the falling leaf
Stretch happy skies ;
With colors and sweet cries
Of mating birds in uplands and in glades
The world is rife.
Then on a sudden all the music dies,
The color fades.
How fugitive and brief
Is mortal life
Between the budding and the falling leaf !

O short-breathed music, dying on the
    tongue
Ere half the mystic canticle be sung !
O harp of life, so speedily unstrung !
Who, if 't were his to choose, would
    know again
The bitter sweetness of the lost refrain,
Its rapture, and its pain ?

II

Though I be shut in darkness, and be-
　　come
Insentient dust blown idly here and there,
I count oblivion a scant price to pay
For having once had held against my lip
Life's brimming cup of hydromel and
　　rue —
For having once known woman's holy
　　love
And a child's kiss, and for a little space
Been boon companion to the Day and
　　Night,
Fed on the odors of the summer dawn,
And folded in the beauty of the stars.
Dear Lord, though I be changed to
　　senseless clay,
And serve the potter as he turns his
　　wheel,
I thank Thee for the gracious gift of
　　tears!

XXXVIII

ANDALUSIAN CRADLE-SONG

(FROM " MERCEDES ")

Who is it opens her blue bright eye,
Bright as the sea and blue as the sky ? —
   Chiquita !
Who has the smile that comes and goes
Like sunshine over her mouth's red
  rose ? —
   Muchachita !

What is the softest laughter heard,
Gurgle of brook or trill of bird,
   Chiquita ?
Nay, 't is thy laughter makes the rill
Hush its voice and the bird be still,
   Muchachita !

Ah, little flower-hand on my breast,
How it soothes me and gives me rest !
   Chiquita !

What is the sweetest sight I know?
Three little white teeth in a row,
Three little white teeth in a row,
  Muchachita!

THE VOICE OF THE SEA

In the hush of the autumn night
I hear the voice of the sea,
In the hush of the autumn night
It seems to say to me —
Mine are the winds above,
Mine are the caves below,
Mine are the dead of yesterday
And the dead of long ago !

And I think of the fleet that sailed
From the lovely Gloucester shore,
I think of the fleet that sailed
And came back nevermore ;
My eyes are filled with tears,
And my heart is numb with woe —
It seems as if 't were yesterday,
And it all was long ago !

XL

"I VEX ME NOT WITH BROOD-
ING ON THE YEARS "

I VEX me not with brooding on the years
That were ere I drew breath : why should
    I then
Distrust the darkness that may fall again
When life is done ?   Perchance in other
    spheres —
Dead planets — I once tasted mortal
    tears,
And walked as now among a throng of
    men,
Pondering things that lay beyond my
    ken,
Questioning death, and solacing my fears.
Ofttimes indeed strange sense have I of
    this,
Vague memories that hold me with a
    spell,
Touches of unseen lips upon my brow,

Breathing some incommunicable bliss !
In years foregone, O Soul, was all not
   well ?
Still lovelier life awaits thee.   Fear not
   thou !

XLI

A SERENADE

I

Imp of Dreams, when she 's asleep,
To her snowy chamber creep,
And straight whisper in her ear
What, awake, she will not hear —
    Imp of Dreams, when she 's asleep.

II

Tell her, so she may repent,
That no rose withholds its scent,
That no bird that has a song
Hoards the music summer-long —
    Tell her, so she may repent.

III

Tell her there 's naught else to do,
If to-morrow's skies be blue,
But to come, with civil speech,
And walk with me to Hampton Beach —

Tell her there 's naught else to do!
  Tell her, so she may repent —
    Imp of Dreams, when she 's asleep!

A REFRAIN

HIGH in a tower she sings,
  I, passing by beneath,
Pause and listen, and catch
  These words of passionate breath —
" *Asphodel, flower of Life ; amaranth,*
   flower of Death ! "

Sweet voice, sweet unto tears !
  What is this that she saith ?
Poignant, mystical — hark !
  Again, with passionate breath —
" *Asphodel, flower of Life ; amaranth,*
   flower of Death ! "

"GREAT CAPTAIN, GLORIOUS IN OUR WARS"

GREAT Captain, glorious in our wars —
No meed of praise we hold from him;
About his brow we wreathe the stars
The coming ages shall not dim.

The cloud-sent man! Was it not he
That from the hand of adverse fate
Snatched the white flower of victory?
He spoke no word, but saved the State.

Yet History, as she brooding bends
Above the tablet on her knee,
The impartial stylus half suspends,
And fain would blot the cold decree:

"The iron hand and sleepless care
That stayed disaster scarce availed
To save him when he came to wear
The civic laurel: there he failed."

Who runs may read ; but nothing mars
That nobler record, unforgot.
Great Captain, glorious in our wars —
All else the heart remembers not.

REMINISCENCE

THOUGH I am native to this frozen zone
That half the twelvemonth torpid lies, or
  dead;
Though the cold azure arching overhead
And the Atlantic's never-ending moan
Are mine by heritage, I must have known
Life otherwhere in epochs long since fled;
For in my veins some Orient blood is red,
And through my thought are lotus blos-
  soms blown.
I do remember . . . it was just at dusk,
Near a walled garden at the river's turn
(A thousand summers seem but yester-
  day!)
A Nubian girl, more sweet than Khoorja
  musk,
Came to the water-tank to fill her urn,
And, with the urn, she bore my heart
  away!

BROKEN MUSIC

A note
All out of tune in this world's instrument.
AMY LEVY.

I KNOW not in what fashion she was
    made,
  Nor what her voice was, when she
    used to speak,
Nor if the silken lashes threw a shade
    On wan or rosy cheek.

I picture her with sorrowful vague eyes
  Illumed with such strange gleams of
    inner light
As linger in the drift of London skies
    Ere twilight turns to night.

I know not; I conjecture. 'T was a girl
  That with her own most gentle desper-
    ate hand

From out God's mystic setting plucked
    life's pearl —
        'T is hard to understand.

So precious life is !   Even to the old
    The hours are as a miser's coins, and
        she —
Within her hands lay youth's unminted
    gold
        And all felicity.

The winged impetuous spirit, the white
    flame
    That was her soul once, whither has it
        flown?
Above her brow gray lichens blot her
    name
        Upon the carven stone.

This is her Book of Verses — wren-like
    notes,
    Shy franknesses, blind gropings, haunt-
        ing fears ;
At times across the chords abruptly floats
        A mist of passionate tears.

A fragile lyre too tensely keyed and
    strung,
A broken music, weirdly incomplete:
Here a proud mind, self-baffled and self-
    stung,
    Lies coiled in dark defeat.

XLVI

COMEDY

THEY parted, with clasps of hand
And kisses, and burning tears.
They met, in a foreign land,
After some twenty years :

Met as acquaintances meet,
Smilingly, tranquil-eyed —
Not even the least little beat
Of the heart, upon either side.

They chatted of this and that,
The nothings that make up life;
She in a Gainsborough hat,
And he in black for his wife.

XLVII

SEEMING DEFEAT

I

THE woodland silence, one time stirred
By the soft pathos of some passing bird,
 Is not the same it was before.
The spot where once, unseen, a flower
Has held its fragile chalice to the shower,
 Is different for evermore.
  Unheard, unseen
  A spell has been!

II

O thou that breathest year by year
Music that falls unheeded on the ear,
 Take heart, fate has not baffled thee!
Thou that with tints of earth and skies

Fillest thy canvas for unseeing eyes,
Thou hast not labored futilely.
Unheard, unseen
A spell has been!

XLVIII

A PETITION

To spring belongs the violet, and the
    blown
Spice of the roses let the summer own.
Grant me this favor, Muse — all else
    withhold —
That I may not write verse when I am
    old.

And yet I pray you, Muse, delay the time!
Be not too ready to deny me rhyme;
And when the hour strikes, as it must,
    dear Muse,
I beg you very gently break the news.

QUITS

If my best wines mislike thy taste,
And my best service win thy frown,
Then tarry not, I bid thee haste ;
There's many another Inn in town.

.

www.ingramcontent.com/pod-product-compliance
Lightning Source LLC
Chambersburg PA
CBHW020258090426
42735CB00009B/1140